COUTURE TAROT

MEGAN SKINNER

4880 Lower Valley Road, Atglen, PA 19310

Copyright © 2025 by Megan Skinner

Library of Congress Control Number: 2024952884

All rights reserved. No part of this work may be reproduced or used in any form or by any means—graphic, electronic, or mechanical, including photocopying or information storage and retrieval systems—without written permission from the publisher.

The scanning, uploading, and distribution of this book or any part thereof via the Internet or any other means without the permission of the publisher is illegal and punishable by law. Please purchase only authorized editions and do not participate in or encourage the electronic piracy of copyrighted materials.

"Red Feather Mind Body Spirit" logo is a trademark of Schiffer Publishing, Ltd.
"Red Feather Mind Body Spirit Feather" logo is a registered trademark of Schiffer Publishing, Ltd.

Designed by Danielle D. Farmer
Type set in NeubauGrotesk/Bookmania/New Farm/Allure
Image Credits: Close up on diamond wedding and engagement rings. Courtesy of BigStock Photography © Eye Full

ISBN: 978-0-7643-6985-8
Printed in China

Published by REDFeather Mind, Body, Spirit
An imprint of Schiffer Publishing, Ltd.
4880 Lower Valley Road
Atglen, PA 19310
Phone: (610) 593-1777; Fax: (610) 593-2002
Email: Info@redfeathermbs.com
Web: www.redfeathermbs.com

For our complete selection of fine books on this and related subjects, please visit our website at www.redfeathermbs.com. You may also write for a free catalog.

REDFeather Mind, Body, Spirit's titles are available at special discounts for bulk purchases for sales promotions or premiums. Special editions, including personalized covers, corporate imprints, and excerpts, can be created in large quantities for special needs. For more information, contact the publisher.

We are always looking for people to write books on new and related subjects. If you have an idea for a book, please contact us at proposals@schifferbooks.com.

MIX
Paper | Supporting responsible forestry
FSC® C005748

Other REDFeather Titles on Related Subjects:

Boadicea's Tarot of Earthly Delights, Caroline Kenner, illustrated by Paula Millet, ISBN 978-0-7643-6908-7

Outsider Art Tarot, Rita Rose and photography and graphic design by Jana Pesek, ISBN 978-0-7643-6270-5

The Zerner/Farber Tarot, Amy Zerner & Monte Farber, ISBN 978-0-7643-6451-8

For my mother,
Sally Jo Langdon Skinner

ACKNOWLEDGMENTS

The *Couture Tarot* would not have been possible without the invaluable contributions of David Thomas, *Couture*'s original designer, whose vision greatly influenced the deck's look and vibe; Darcy Pease, the original editor of the guidebook, for her patience and insight; Zaara Kittenchops, my Tarot soul sister, for her mentorship in manifesting the deck; Stephanie Gailing, for her ongoing encouragement, wisdom, and keen eye; and Rachel Stevens, for guiding and editing the new, expanded guidebook.

I'm also grateful to the wonderful team at REDFeather for giving the *Couture Tarot* a new life, one with the beautiful golden touches it deserves.

CONTENTS

INTRODUCTION	10
ABOUT THE TAROT	12
WORKING WITH THE *Couture Tarot*	13
ENGAGING WITH THE TAROT	14

THE MAJOR ARCANA — 17

- 19 ..... 0 Fool
- 21 ..... I Magician
- 23 ..... II High Priestess
- 25 ..... III Empress
- 27 ..... IV Emperor
- 29 ..... V Hierophant
- 31 ..... VI Lovers
- 33 ..... VII Chariot
- 35 ..... VIII Strength
- 37 ..... IX Hermit
- 39 ..... X Wheel of Fortune
- 41 ..... XI Justice
- 43 ..... XII Hanged Man
- 45 ..... XIII Death
- 47 ..... XIV Temperance
- 49 ..... XV Devil
- 51 ..... XVI Tower
- 53 ..... XVII Star
- 55 ..... XVIII Moon
- 57 ..... XIX Sun
- 59 ..... XX Judgement
- 61 ..... XXI The World

THE MINOR ARCANA

THE SUIT OF WANDS:
FIRE 64

67 .... Ace of Wands
69 .... Two of Wands
71 .... Three of Wands
73 .... Four of Wands
75 .... Five of Wands
77 .... Six of Wands
79 .... Seven of Wands
81 .... Eight of Wands
83 .... Nine of Wands
85 .... Ten of Wands
87 .... Page of Wands
89 .... Knight of Wands
91 .... Queen of Wands
93 .... King of Wands

THE SUIT OF CUPS:
WATER.......................94

97 .... Ace of Cups
99 .... Two of Cups
101 ... Three of Cups
103 ... Four of Cups
105 ... Five of Cups
107 ... Six of Cups
109 ... Seven of Cups
111 ... Eight of Cups
113 ... Nine of Cups
115 ... Ten of Cups
117 ... Page of Cups
119 ... Knight of Cups
121 ... Queen of Cups
123 ... King of Cups

THE SUIT OF SWORDS:
AIR.......................124

127 ... Ace of Swords
129 ... Two of Swords
131 ... Three of Swords
133 ... Four of Swords
135 ... Five of Swords
137 ... Six of Swords
139 ... Seven of Swords
141 ... Eight of Swords
143 ... Nine of Swords
145 ... Ten of Swords
147 ... Page of Swords
149 ... Knight of Swords
151 ... Queen of Swords
153 ... King of Swords

THE SUIT OF PENTACLES:
EARTH.......................154

157 ... Ace of Pentacles
159 ... Two of Pentacles
161 ... Three of Pentacles
163 ... Four of Pentacles
165 ... Five of Pentacles
167 ... Six of Pentacles
169 ... Seven of Pentacles
171 ... Eight of Pentacles
173 ... Nine of Pentacles
175 ... Ten of Pentacles
177 ... Page of Pentacles
179 ... Knight of Pentacles
181 ... Queen of Pentacles
183 ... King of Pentacles

COUTURE TAROT CARD SPREADS 184

INTRODUCTION

I received my first Tarot card deck when I was fourteen years old. From the moment I saw that deck of cards, I was mesmerized, and the Tarot has been my dear companion ever since. Creating my own deck has been a labor of love, and I'm beyond delighted to share it with you. Each of the cards in the *Couture Tarot* was created with my hands through collage art, using images from fashion magazines.

When I was a teenager, my mother and I spent many happy afternoons after school with a cup of tea and Pepperidge Farm gingerbread cookies looking through our preferred magazines: *Vogue*, *Bazaar*, *Elle*, *Glamour*, and *Mademoiselle*. We'd earmark the pages with our favorite outfits, some of which my mother, a seamstress, would re-create.

This thread of love, fashion, and connection is continued in the *Couture Tarot*. To me, high fashion is art, and one of my greatest inspirations. From a stack of fashion magazines, I became a mystical seamstress, cutting and sewing (or, in this case, pasting) together different images to create seventy-eight individual tapestries reflecting the energies of each card.

After a long illness, my mother passed while I was in the process of creating the deck. I know that her presence was with me, whispering and nudging me along as each card came to life. I like to think that as an artist and fashionista in her own right, she would love the result. C'est voilà, Mom!

In this new edition, I have elaborated on each card description to offer deeper and more personal insight. I'm also delighted that the deck is beautifully enhanced with gilded touches. My dearest wish is that this deck whispers to you through insight and inspiration, prompting your imagination toward knowledge and self-discovery. May it lead you to discover your own unique sense of the Tarot.

With love,
Megan

ABOUT THE TAROT

The Tarot is experiencing an exciting renaissance, with many new decks and interpretations available. I believe this is because its wisdom is timeless; like a shape-shifter, its archetypes are constantly transforming, reflecting both ancient and current zeitgeists, the fashion of the time.

The power of the Tarot, its great magic, is that it imparts its wisdom through pictures and images. Unlike words, symbols and archetypes bypass the conscious mind and connect to deeper levels of your psyche. In the best sense, the Tarot offers a reflection, a mirror, into your deeper mind and soul. With intention, you will find that each card of the deck has the potential to illuminate different aspects of your life and bring answers to your most-compelling questions.

To fully engage with the Tarot, you must be willing to explore the mystery. At times its revelations will be completely apparent, an "Aha!" moment, but at others the realizations are more elusive. The Tarot is a visual poetry, filled with mystical metaphors and allegories, inspiring greater thought. Ultimately, the Tarot is an intuitive oracle, one that encourages you to use your imagination and deeper perspective to discern the meanings.

WORKING WITH
THE *Couture Tarot*

The art for each card of the *Couture Tarot* is rooted in traditional symbolism with a modern twist, created through collage by using images from current fashion magazines. Collage art is defined as "bringing diverse elements together in an unlikely or unexpected juxtaposition." And so it is for the *Couture Tarot*! Some of the cards may look familiar, especially to those with a knowledge of the Tarot. Others, at first measure, may seem less familiar but awaken a new perspective.

This is especially true in the cards of the Minor Arcana, which do not necessarily include the actual symbol of the suit (i.e., Wands, Cups, Swords, and Pentacles), as in a traditional deck. Yet, each image carries the essence of the suit and card through color and a visual story.

I have included an astrological association, a ruler for each card. Assigning a zodiac sign or planet to the cards came into vogue in the early twentieth century, most notably through the work of the

Golden Dawn, a mystical organization that used the Tarot as a means for illumination and spiritual development.

It can be helpful to learn through association, and there are parallels between different systems of mystical knowledge and the Tarot. Most notably, numerology, the Kabbalah, and astrology, which can apply to your understanding of the cards. As an astrologer, I especially love to explore the astrological associations. If the astrological element doesn't speak to you, know that it is not essential to your understanding. They are simply reference points and fun to explore for those astrologically minded.

ENGAGING WITH THE TAROT

There are different ways to engage with the Tarot. Perhaps the most potent is to ask a question and then choose one card to reflect the answer. By spending time with the card, answers will be revealed, bringing more clarity to your situation. Sometimes even in surprising ways! Exploring each card individually can be quite profound. For example, applying meditation and journaling to your process will bring more nuance and deeper insight. Personally, I like to pull a card every few days or so to see what wisdom the Universe wants to bring to my attention.

Another way to utilize the Tarot is through doing readings by using different card spreads. There are many different spreads to choose from, from a simple three-card layout (past, present, future), to the traditional more in-depth Celtic Cross spread. You can find several *Couture Tarot* card spreads, including the Celtic Cross, at the end of this guidebook starting on p. 184.

As you explore the cards of the Tarot, it's important to remember that because the Tarot is based in the language of symbols and archetypes, its wisdom is open to interpretation. This guidebook offers definitions for each card and is meant to be a starting point for your own discovery. If my interpretation does not resonate with you, then allow your intuition to guide you to a more personal or relevant understanding.

Finally, I am not a believer in the concept of right-side up / positive meanings versus reversed cards / negative meanings. I feel that this is portending in nature, alluding to fate and defined outcomes. I would offer a more holistic approach: that each card holds the energies of both light and shadow. This perspective gives a more nuanced picture of each that allows for deeper explanation. In the best sense, the cards of the Tarot are insightful cues to living a more evolved life.

for megan

x strapped upon the feet,
holding up the weak.
in the void of
all transmissions,
in the ethers xxx in the
glow,
the fabric of eternal
   situation the

THE MAJOR ARCANA

There are two books, or sections, to a Tarot deck: the Major Arcana and the Minor Arcana. The Major Arcana is the spiritual foundation of the Tarot. Some, including myself, believe that it was created separately, before the Minor Arcana, in the Mystery Schools of ancient Egypt. Each of the twenty-two cards of the Major Arcana represents a different spiritual lesson, offering the potential for greater awareness and a deeper understanding to your life journey.

0 FOOL

KEYWORDS

Fearlessness, innocence, divine madness, inspiration, freedom, rebellion, risk-taking, quantum leaps

RULER: Uranus

The Fool indicates major and exciting change—offering a quantum leap forward in your life! This is a time to be open to grand new possibilities. The Fool is a rebel, defying limitations to create his life in big, bold strokes, and never hesitating to color outside the lines. He can take on many different personas, most notably that of jester and divine trickster. I chose a fox for the *Couture*'s Fool, since in animal symbolism the fox is associated with trickster energy. Here, our Fool is an avant-garde fox wearing a pinstriped suit, with a butterfly bow tie. Daring choice? Absolutely! But that is how the Fool rolls, bravely and joyously, without a care about what anyone may think.

The Fool is a compelling force, encouraging you to fearlessly act on what inspires you. Is he crazy, or divinely inspired? Perhaps both! Either way, you are being called and must take the leap. There is no guarantee of outcomes, but if you are willing to risk his folly, dancing with the Fool ensures that you will never be the same again!

I MAGICIAN

KEYWORDS

Beginnings, learning, discipline, intention, manifestation, willpower, communication, mindfulness

RULER: Mercury

The Magician, not the Fool, is the first card of the deck. The Fool travels through the deck as we do, a wandering holy vagabond. The Magician represents beginnings and creation. Ruled by Mercury, the winged messenger of the gods, the Magician connects you with your innate "god" power: the ability to manifest your ideas into reality. Here, you are the creator, the very architect of your life. I put the *Couture*'s Magician in Vegas-style tux, cape, sleight of hand, and a rabbit pulled from a hat. We also see a monkey and the Eye of Horus, both connected to the Egyptian deity Thoth. Thoth is the god of writing, science, art, and magic. Behind the Magician is a golden pyramid, a reservoir of ancient power and secrets. They are at any Magician's disposal. You just need to be a willing adept.

The key to the Magician's power lies in the ability to focus his mind. To exert his will. Mind over matter. This requires you to be fully present to each moment. Your intentions, your thoughts, your words all carry energy and are extremely powerful now. Set them with care and let them be your focus, without distraction.

II HIGH PRIESTESS

KEYWORDS

Intuition, reflection, stillness, darkness, wisdom, sacred feminine, soul, spiritual mother

RULER: The Moon

The High Priestess is the spiritual mother, keeper of eternal knowledge. She is associated with the sacred feminine, representing the gifts of intuition, compassion, and deep wisdom. She is a reminder of your own innate wisdom and calls you to go within, to commune with the infinite well of your soul. The poem in this card came from a street artist, who was writing poems based on a single word. I was working on the High Priestess at the time, so I chose the word "soul." To me, his poem carries the essence of the High Priestess.

For Megan
Strapped upon the feet, holding up the weak,
In the void of all transmissions, in the ethers,
In the glow,
The fabric of eternal situation the
Orchestration of the flow,
The burning sun as
Like the one,
That changes with the breeze …
Holding on to nothing much
Except what we cannot see

Remember, the soul/intuitive realm doesn't always appear in a linear manner. It requires the patience and fortitude to go within, into the unknown mystery. It is in the dark reaches of your psyche where your answers lie. This is a time for reflection and introspection. Let your intuition guide you to what you need to know.

III EMPRESS

KEYWORDS

Love, creativity, wisdom, pleasure, beauty, abundance, heart, earth mother

RULER: Venus

The Empress is a divinely sensual creature. She is the embodiment of love, both in its earthly and celestial forms. The Empress is in full bloom—sated, accomplished, and realized. The Empress is associated with Mother Nature. Here, she is surrounded by a few of nature's most exquisite creations: roses, berries, and butterflies. A shower of diamonds fall around her, a gem esteemed for its beauty and purity. A Queen of Hearts, she wears a crown of antlers, indicating her connection not only to the flora of Earth, but also her fauna. Finally, her crown holds a single star showing her connection to the Divine.

The Empress has experienced the richness of life, and its perpetual give and take. She is comfortable in her own skin, which is the essence of true beauty. As a result, many are attracted to her luminosity and abundant embrace. This is a time to explore how you wish to experience love. As you value yourself and your loving gifts, you create more-fulfilling relationships.

IV EMPEROR

KEYWORDS

Authority, empowerment, realization, foundations, responsibility, leadership, confidence, earth father

RULER: Aries

The Emperor indicates empowerment, a time when you are fully realizing your personal power in the world. This is especially true careerwise, since you are building important foundations for the future. This Emperor doesn't wear armor or carry a sword. Instead, he wears a bespoke suit and tie just like the businessman—the king of enterprise—he is. Sharply dressed, he exudes power and confidence. He's not here to fight, but to fully embody who he is. You know he's on top of his game, because he owns it—completely.

The Emperor is a born leader, confident and self-assured. As a result, others look to him for leadership. Yet, the mantel of authority can be a heavy crown, for it also brings responsibility. This is a time when you are considering how you wield your power in the world. When out of balance, the Emperor becomes a dictator, a negative authority figure. Keep your ego in check and conquer your future with a benevolent heart.

V HIEROPHANT

KEYWORDS

Tradition, community, leadership, knowledge, teaching, faith, divine abundance, spiritual father

RULER: Taurus

The Hierophant represents the spiritual father, the person we look to for guidance and higher knowledge. He is our earthly connection to the Divine, with a focus on tradition and sacred community. The *Couture*'s Hierophant was inspired by the idea of the Three Wise Men who followed the Star of Bethlehem to the birth of the Christ Child. Some say these Wise Men were Persian astrologers who used their knowledge, combined with faith, to reach their destination. They are surrounded by stacks of writings, pages upon pages of holy scripture; an invitation to share your own knowledge with others and to look for establishments of higher learning for greater answers.

In the highest sense, the Hierophant provides a stable foundation, leading you on a path toward revelation and greater faith. This is a time to find your voice and share your spiritual truth with others. The gifts of spirit are plentiful. The more you value your connection with the Divine, the more you will see it all around you. In others, in miracles, and in acts of grace. Appreciating this is the mark of a true spiritual being. Lead by example.

VI LOVERS

KEYWORDS

Discernment, choice, relationship, crossroads, commitment, learning, wholeness, alchemical marriage

RULER: Gemini

The Lovers indicates a relationship crossroads, after the proverbial honeymoon and the high of romantic love settles. Our Lovers embrace, surrounded by a lush, potentially dangerous landscape. It is a time when you are making choices about your future through the relationships in your life. This is not about fate but, rather, free will. Discernment is key. Ask yourself: Am I ready to commit fully to this relationship? If not, it's time to move on. Our lovers are mirrors, offering opportunities to learn about our deepest selves. In the choices we make, we learn, grow, and even transform. Ultimately, the Lovers card will guide you toward an inner union, creating a wholeness within. Mystics call this the alchemical marriage.

I was inspired by a New Orleans backdrop, hot and steamy, florid and exotic. The woman in the foreground is a madam, the proprietor of sexual delights. A passion flower, serpentlike, tempts the Lovers from above, with an array of enticing apples below. Much like Adam and Eve, the Lovers have a choice to make. Innocence or knowledge? Whatever your choices, bite into them with the passion they deserve.

VII CHARIOT

KEYWORDS

Ambition, action, intuition, success, forward movement, beginnings, achievement, self-realization

RULER: Cancer

The Chariot is a journey of self-realization, as you begin to embody your dreams and desires, filled with the ambition to make them real. Where else would the Chariot come from, but the sea! The watery domain of the soul, dreams, and unconscious desires. The *Couture*'s Charioteer is a sea goddess. She is split between the "real world" and the sea and has found a balance between the two. Her head is that of a horse, usually one of the animals leading the Chariot as it charges into action.

The Chariot is described as a movement of the soul, for on this voyage you take charge of your destiny, with your intuition to guide you. Gather your courage and go after your goals! There is no game plan, for it would only limit you. The Chariot reminds us that no matter the destination, what is important is the journey itself. This is an opportunity to define your character in the face of unknown elements, and even adversity, while staying true to yourself. The Chariot's voyage ahead is filled with many unknowns, but it is her strong sense of self and inner strength that allows her to safely travel forward.

VIII STRENGTH

KEYWORDS

Passion, union, innocence, grace, patience, vulnerability, surrender, self-love

RULER: Leo

The Strength card is associated with the fairy tale *Beauty and the Beast*... Once upon a time, a maiden encountered a ferocious lion! Her first instinct was to run away. Instead, the innocent maiden decided to befriend the beast. Gently and patiently, she got to know the lion, ultimately falling in love. In return, the lion surrendered to her. The lion represents desire—which can be one scary beast! Here, strength comes in vulnerability, as you give yourself permission to fall in love with yourself—thorns and all.

In the whimsical spirit of a fairy tale, our maiden is portrayed as a pretty layer cake in the *Couture*'s Strength card. The cake represents her innocence and sweetness—suggesting that you *can* have your cake and eat it too! The lion courts her with flowers, a notion of his surrender. They are enveloped in a landscape of decadent blooms—some wild, some cultivated—indicating the potential pleasures inherent to this card. Consider lifestyle changes benefiting a more authentic you. Don't force anything. Be sweet with yourself. Patience—inner strength—is your ally.

IX HERMIT

KEYWORDS

Faith, inner journey, path, solitude, wisdom, self-discovery, guidance, mystic

RULER: Virgo

The Hermit is an old soul. A mysterious creature, he is a loner traveling through an unknown forest. His journey is at twilight, that magical time when the veils between worlds, light and dark, are most transparent. Traveling here requires faith, the knowledge that there is always a star to guide and light your way. The road to wisdom can be a difficult path, for true wisdom comes from the hard lessons and experience of time and usually time alone. In my rendition of this card, a merlin perches on the Hermit's arm. The merlin is associated with visionary powers, wisdom, and guardianship. This small but powerful hawk is said to lead one to their life purpose. A reminder that even though it may feel that way, you are never alone when seeking the Divine. Guidance comes in many different forms.

The Hermit calls you to embark upon a solitary yet profound journey of self-discovery. You are seeking your true path, which comes from within. You may need to disconnect from the outer world in order to focus inward. This is a mystic's journey.

X WHEEL of FORTUNE

KEYWORDS

Change, opportunity, expansion, fortune, serendipity, flexibility, centeredness, eternal flow

RULER: Jupiter

Life is change, and change is life. The Wheel of Fortune, like life itself, can be a rollercoaster ride! One minute up, the next down. The Wheel of Fortune looks to be a roulette wheel housed within a very expensive watch. A flamingo, the animal totem representing balance and stability, centers the wheel as it spins round and round in a whirl of possibilities. It is the flamingo's stability that allows the participant to expand into unknown futures, without being touched by the wheel's perpetual ups and downs. Creating your own luck sometimes is as simple as being open to unexpected gifts and opportunities, and life's serendipities.

Flexibility is key. Letting go of attachment to outcomes will help you find centeredness and place you in the eternal flow. The more you go outside your comfort zones, the more possibilities you will find. Be excited about the opportunities ahead; things are happening fast! A well-lived life is one where you take chances. Be a willing gambler and spin the wheel, then let the chips fall where they may. You are successful for just showing up and playing the game!

XI JUSTICE

KEYWORDS

Balance, equilibrium, adjustment, truth, inner peace, center, discernment, wisdom

RULER: Libra

Justice indicates a pivotal moment—a time to realign with your essential truth. Wisdom comes from knowing what is true and right. This is a continual process of adjustment, of weighing and measuring to discern what is working and not working in your life. In a snowy winter forest, Lady Justice merges with the form of an owl. She wears a beautiful crystal crown housing the scales of justice perfectly balanced. The owl is able to see in the darkness and is connected with the goddess Athena, the goddess of wisdom and truth. The cold landscape indicates that this is not warm or emotionally fulfilling territory. Instead, it is a place of looking clearly at the facts.

Justice requires that you remain focused and do not waver in your examination. Getting to the truth of matters requires concentration and mental stillness. Your newfound clarity will lighten your heart and bring inner peace. Pay attention to situations that throw you out of balance. Whenever possible, avoid extremes and continue to regain your center. Harmony comes from maintaining a state of equilibrium within.

XII HANGED MAN

KEYWORDS

Suspension, surrender, new perspective, perfectionism, illusion, martyrdom, faith, divine right timing

RULER: Neptune

The Hanged Man is in a state of suspension. Once his feet were on the ground—representing a material, earthbound reality; now they are in the air—indicating that he has surrendered to a higher or spiritual reality. Our Hanged Man has truly let go, to the point of falling off a rocky cliff into the ocean! The ocean alludes to the card's astrological ruler, Neptune, the god of the ocean, and on a spiritual level, the place where we all merge into one. The Hanged Man has surrendered but is not defeated. The yellow songbird is a witness to his action.

The Hanged Man is choosing to relinquish control, to open himself to a new perspective. He has let go of perfectionism, realizing it is an illusion, impossible to fulfill. The Hanged Man reminds that you are never the victim of circumstances, and warns against defeatism or playing the martyr. You have choices, even if that means learning to trust the flow. Embrace divine right timing, knowing that spirit will take care of you. If there was ever a time to let go and let "god"—this would be it.

XIII DEATH

KEYWORDS

Endings, completion, fear, unknown, transformation, internal change, liberation, surrender

RULER: Scorpio

Death represents profound endings. This process may come in different stages: fear, anger, denial, bargaining, grief, and acceptance. Here, Death's head is a clock, representing Kronos or Father Time, reminding us of the ephemeral nature of life. Inspiration for the *Couture*'s Death came from a Leonard Cohen song, "Famous Blue Raincoat." One of my favorite songs. I like to think that when death comes, she will be wearing a leather "blue raincoat... torn at the shoulder... with a rose in her teeth, a thin gypsy thief." The song was written as a letter from his brother that is filled with anger, sadness, grief, and the longing of days past.

Like a dark angel, Death always hovers, warning that, one way or another, all things must come to their completion. The Tarot's Death rarely indicates a physical one; instead its transformation is more internal, that of a spiritual, emotional, or psychological nature. Embracing death can give greater meaning to your life. It liberates. For if you fear death, you cannot be present to living your life to the fullest.

XIV TEMPERANCE

KEYWORDS

Balance, learning, art, experimentation, integration, creativity, alchemical marriage, transformation

RULER: Sagittarius

Temperance represents a new balance as you integrate different elements of your life—symbolized in this card as silver (the Moon) and gold (the Sun). When these opposite forces are mixed together, a divine alchemy occurs, transforming them into something completely new and powerful. For the *Couture*'s Temperance, I envisioned an alchemist's workshop from time past: crucibles, crosses, compasses, mathematical rulers, ethereal trapped lovers, plant essences, the tree of life, and an angel. Time to mix, conjure, transmute, and experiment!

Temperance is associated with the art of alchemy, a symbolic process of turning lead into gold. This is a time to elevate yourself through learning experiences, ones that appeal to your higher aesthetic. Be creative and experiment with different possibilities. The angels are watching over you, guiding your quest for knowledge, making sure it aligns with your greatest good. Life is the greatest experiment, and learning something new is the ultimate golden treasure.

XV DEVIL

KEYWORDS

Fear, obsession, control, desire, power struggles, creativity, transmutation, dark side

RULER: Capricorn

This Devil is both sexy and frightening! As it should be, for it is an awakening of your cardinal desires, deepest passions, and creative instincts. Like a poisonous snakebite, this will either kill, enslaving you to your obsessions and fear-based behaviors, or bring healing as you learn to transmute these energies in a healthy way. This is powerful, creative medicine! The Tree of Knowledge holds the forbidden fruit, the serpent intertwined within its roots. Temptation awaits! Yet, the tree also shows the all-seeing eye, a symbol for wisdom and seeing beyond illusion into what is real. The serpent is connected with kundalini energy—the procreative life force that circulates through the body via the chakra system. Kundalini is often associated with the sacred Feminine.

The Devil card has nothing to do with evil; rather, it's calling you to explore your dark side: the parts of yourself that bring fear or make you feel out of control. There is power in your darkness. Make friends with your demons and bring them into the light of self-acceptance!

XVI TOWER

KEYWORDS

Death, destruction, dismantling, foundations, clearing, healing, rebirth, liberation

RULER: Mars

The Tower is falling, or, more accurately, it is self-destructing, a fiery devastation of its former existence. Its falling, or failing, comes because its structures are too weak to hold the weight of a coming new reality. In ancient literature the Tower is associated with the Tower of Babel and the sin of hubris. The Tower indicates a death, a time when certain structures of your life are being dismantled to make way for something newly evolved. This can be a painful process, but, still, you must let go. This is not a time for rebuilding, for you would only be re-creating outlived structures. For now, surrender and use this time to grieve and heal. Then, the Phoenix shall rise from the ashes once again!

Like the phoenix, shown in the *Couture*'s Tower as a fiery purple bird, also rises the Star, our next arcanum. Something to keep in mind as you're experiencing the Tower: know that it's the Tower's very destruction that liberates you to expand into the Star's higher realms of inspiration and destiny. Don't let fear of change or your ego get in the way.

XVII STAR

KEYWORDS

Inspiration imagination, destiny, dreams, manifestation, luminary, faith, "as above, so below"

RULER: Aquarius

The Star holds a universe of unlimited potentials, just waiting to be explored! Now is the time to manifest your dreams into reality. The goddess Nuit, Our Lady of the Stars, glides through the cosmic skies, past planets and stars, in a magical teacup and saucer. Her watering can is ready to sprinkle the heavenly jewels of inspirations, dreams, and higher potentials upon the earth. An inspiration for the *Couture*'s Star comes from the Langston Hughes poem "Dream Dust":

> *Gather out of star-dust,*
>   *Earth dust, Cloud-dust, Storm-dust,*
> *And Splinters of hail, one handful of dream-dust,*
>   *Not for sale.*

The Star asks that you reach high, cast your net wide, and be willing to explore different possibilities. Your dreams and wishes are not flights of fancy; they are divine callings to your future. Believe and have confidence as you align with your greater destiny. Pay attention to what inspires you. This will guide you forward. As you reach for your stars, you elevate your life and become a shining light for others to follow.

XVIII MOON

KEYWORDS

Shadow, reflection, bewitchment, the past, deception, mystery, unresolved emotions, illumination

RULER: Pisces

The Moon is a compelling presence; she is as old as time, a seductress, bewitching us with her shadowy light. Lady Luna casts illusions, asking us to consider what is real and what is not. "*When the moon hits your eye like a big pizza pie—that's amore!*" The Moon came to me in a New York City landscape, reminiscent of the movie *Moonstruck*. An ode to romantic lunacy and what a little moonlight can do. The plate and spoon come from the nursery rhyme ("and the cow jumped over the moon"). The dog is Anubis, the Egyptian guide dog to the underworld. The Wolf represents our primal wildness—a reminder that sometimes we need to howl at the moon.

Unresolved emotions and fears clouding your thinking, distracting you from what needs to be resolved. The Moon card tells you that this is a time to go within and reflect on the elements of your life that need more illumination. It's easy to get lost in the darkness. In this mysterious landscape, you may need guidance to help you find your way. This is magical territory. New clarity comes as you bring light to the deepest reaches of your psyche.

XIX SUN

KEYWORDS

Light, birth, innocence, freedom, joy, success, vitality, self-expression

RULER: The Sun

The Sun is the most joyful card of the deck! By looking at its bright and powerful imagery, one can't help but feel a sense of expansiveness. The Sun symbolizes birth, a freedom from the weight and shadows of the past. The Sun encourages self-expression, a time to share your light with the world, without worrying about what others may think. Everyone has their own unique gifts, and it's your turn to shine. You're radiating a healthy vitality—let your enthusiasm fill the air! Embrace each day with a childlike innocence and enjoy each moment. Success lies in you being you. Don't make life complicated. The energy of the Sun is simple and pure.

The Sun is the life giver of our solar system. All planets orbit around it, and without its light we would be lost to the darkness. In astrology the Sun represents one's true essence, the individual light that is solely your own. It is important for the Sun to fulfill its light, or individual expression, in order to be truly happy and whole. Never feel selfish when it comes to sharing your gifts. It is your cosmic duty.

XX JUDGEMENT

KEYWORDS

Awakening, accountability, reckoning, truth, integrity, rebirth, liberation, grace

RULER: Pluto

The Judgement card is a wake-up call, heralding a time for major change. This requires an accounting, an assessment of an important matter in your life. In my Judgement card, a fallen angel kneels, praying for redemption. The broken sky above shows there is no going back. What is done is done. The angel is surrounded by willing ancestors—protective witnesses, offering grace and compassion in this defining moment. Stand! Arise! Transform your brokenness and regret into something new and powerful. Time to forgive yourself. All else comes from there.

Ultimately, Judgement is a reckoning as you get to the truth. By doing so, you will experience a profound sense of liberation! This card is a reminder that it is never too late to make a change. Allow for grace. This is soul work as you purify and rise anew. Don't walk away from this moment; act with intention and integrity. Judgement, however, should not be placed upon others. Your process is between you and your angels. The same goes for everyone.

XXI THE WORLD

KEYWORDS

Completion, big picture, travel, leadership, empowerment, manifestation, identity, world ambassador

RULER: Saturn

The World is the last card of the Major Arcana, symbolizing that you have completed its lessons, and now it is time to take all that you've learned and put it out into the world. This card says that you have everything you need to make your mark. This achievement also means that you are now responsible for your creations—big and small. You stand centered in a powerful balance of knowledge and experience. From here you can see the big picture, calling you to step up and lead the way. Whether in your career, self-expression, or global concerns, remember that you are an ambassador for the world. I included a rhinoceros in the *Couture*'s World, because in African folklore the rhinoceros embodies the traits of courage, determination, and wisdom. It is considered a protector of the land and its people.

I've always appreciated the definition that often comes with this card: "The World is your oyster!" And, I would add: "So what do you want to do with it?" The World is both a completion and new beginning rolled into one. In a sense, you get to take your wisdom and play it forward.

THE MINOR ARCANA

The remaining fifty-six cards of the Tarot are the Minor Arcana. Much like a deck of playing cards, they come in four suits: Wands, which represent Fire; Cups, which represent Water; Swords, which represent Air; and Pentacles, which represent Earth. In playing cards the suits correspond to Clubs for Wands, Hearts for Cups, Spades for Swords, and Diamonds for Pentacles. Whereas the Major Arcana focuses on greater, spiritual understandings, the Minor Arcana relates more to the inner workings of your everyday life. Both arcana are important, offering different illumination. You could look at it this way: the Major Arcana is the bigger picture, and the Minor Arcana represents the characters and plot points within that bigger picture.

THE SUIT OF WANDS:
FIRE

The Shakespearean notion that all the world is a stage and we are players in the drama is an appropriate analogy for the suit of Wands. Wands are the element of Fire. They represent spirit in the body—our life force—the desire and passion to become and actively participate in the great drama of human existence. Fire is the spark of light that is your true self and your unique individuality. Wands represent the "fire in your belly" that people speak of when they talk about passion. Wands are dynamic, creative, and expressive. Through the suit of Wands, we experience growth and the evolution of self.

ACE of WANDS

KEYWORDS

Primal energy, birth, creativity, individuality, will, breakthroughs, self-expression

RULER: The element of Fire

The Ace of Wands is one of the most dynamic cards of the deck, since it represents the unleashing of pure, primal fire! Like a volcanic eruption, the seeds of self that have been buried deep within are breaking through into the light of day. The dictations of the past cannot stop this fiery flow of self-awakening. The Ace of Wands is pictured as a very old tree, perhaps dying. Look closely and you will see new leaves and buds beginning to sprout from its limbs. A glimpse of a gray-blue sky arises in the background. The Tree, or Ace, is surrounded by a violent burst of bright colors: pink, orange, and yellow, signaling a breakthrough from the dull, staid colors of the past.

The Ace of Wands represents a highly creative time, as you find yourself newly inspired to express yourself to the world. This powerful awakening is a force that cannot be denied, laying the groundwork for a whole new landscape. Spirit is actively moving through you, as you feel compelled to create a more authentic life.

TWO of WANDS

KEYWORDS

Dominion, forging, fortification, centeredness, self-mastery, strength, divine timing

RULER: Mars in Aries

The great inner fire ignited through the Ace of Wands gathers energy and momentum in the Two of Wands. Now it needs to be focused and stabilized. An analogy is the ancient art of forging iron, the process of shaping and strengthening metal through the heat of flame. The columns and structures, formations of strength and longevity, dominate the image. In fact, Roman columns were a principal structural element in ancient architecture. This is a time to root into your current "infrastructure." Any cracks in the foundation come from self-doubt. Perseverance is the name of the game. If you're looking for courage, put on your favorite outfit or shoes. In this case I chose fabulous lavender shoes, ones with daisy ribbing on top!

You may feel the impulse to conquer new horizons, but here the warrior becomes king, choosing to harness his creative powers for another day. This is self-mastery. You are preparing and fortifying yourself for what is ahead. Center yourself and then, when the time is right, you will be more than ready to act.

THREE of WANDS

KEYWORDS

Virtue, individuality, truth, confidence, power, vitality, integrity

RULER: Sun in Aries

You stand strong, having established a new sense of confidence and individuality. Your presence exudes vitality, and your courageous spirit abounds. This is the moment to bask in your light! At the same time, resist from giving in to prideful or arrogant behavior. It will not serve you and is contrary to the virtuous nature of this card. Focus on the opportunities unfolding. The choices ahead must be aligned with your whole self: body, mind, and spirit—no compromises. Be careful about giving your power away. You have worked hard for this moment. Find strength in your newfound wisdom and remain true to your purpose, separate from the agendas of others.

As you make choices for your future, it is important not to get ahead of yourself (i.e., not to make change for the sake of change). After all, it's not that you don't have what you need, right? Now, it's more about what you want. Time for clear ambitions and goals, knowing that there may be a process involved. Do not see blocks or delays as misalignment, but as divine right timing.

FOUR of WANDS

KEYWORDS

Accomplishment, unity, enjoyment, celebration, heart, harmony, foundations

RULER: Venus in Aries

This joyful card indicates that you have accomplished something wonderful; now it's time to relish in your creations and the satisfaction that comes from a job well done! This card is like a perfect summer day. Sitting in the shade with your best doggie friends, breathing in the fragrant summer air, and relaxing into the comfort of home and family. Sometimes the hardest part of life is taking time to actually enjoy it! This is a moment to let things go for a while. Stretch your legs. Fill up the well. And, most especially, enjoy the company of your dear ones.

Although current conditions may be temporary, they are no less important. By appreciating today, you set up your future on a positive note. Troubled relationships have the opportunity to ease, since you are willing to resolve old conflicts with an open heart. As you embody your success, it frees you to recognize the accomplishments of others. An atmosphere of mutual respect flourishes and everyone is enlivened. Breathe deeply and smell the sweetness of your roses. Celebrate!

FIVE of WANDS

KEYWORDS

Strife, obstacles, chaos, change, creativity, evolution, self-growth

RULER: Saturn in Leo

The number five indicates change, which often manifests through chaos. In the Five of Wands, chaos becomes a valuable part of your creative process, just as change is an important part of self-growth. One of the dangers of this card is becoming overwhelmed to the point of being lost in the process. Here, there's a lot of big, colorful creative energy flying around! And, by knowing this is not the moment to pin things down, let it free your heart and mind to dance with unexpected muses and possibilities. Don't sweat the details, but do keep your bigger goals in mind.

When the Five of Wands shows up, do not try to control the forces at work. Instead dig in, immerse yourself, and evolve! Then you will be able to use what is happening to your advantage. Although obstacles may seem insurmountable, ultimately they are just a bump in the road on your path to destiny. As you continue to grow, like a butterfly you will emerge from the cocoon of your old self, ready to take flight. For now, take life one day at a time.

SIX of WANDS

KEYWORDS

Victory, breakthroughs, confidence, courage, recognition, self-esteem, leadership

RULER: Jupiter in Leo

In the Six of Wands, the stars align and the benevolent forces of the Universe are calling your name. Victory is at hand! It's time to gather your courage and leave the clouds of the past behind. Be proud of your accomplishments and have confidence in your abilities. Others are looking to you for leadership. Now is the time to make your move, as your heart seeks greater recognition. You have worked for this moment and deserve to be acknowledged. The more that you put yourself out there, the more that others can see your worth. This is an excellent time to set goals and put them into action.

In the race of life, you have bet on the winning horse. So, what's the hesitation? Call it what you will—luck, hard work, or divine right timing—the forces are with you. Saddle up, put on your crown, and go for what you really what. I often describe this card as "Follow or get out of my way!"

SEVEN of WANDS

KEYWORDS

Resistance, confrontation, valor, conviction, risk-taking, honesty, authority

RULER: Mars in Leo

The Seven of Wands finds you confronted by resistance, projections, and the expectations of others. Stand your ground! As you embrace your inner warrior, you are filled with courage and a willingness to take risks. As a result, you may find that you are more available to share yourself in an honest and open way. Your presence has impact! As you assert your authority, it's important that your actions are aligned with your best self. As you realize that the opinions of others are simply projections, then, like Alice in Wonderland, you can exclaim, "You're nothing but a deck of cards!" and break free from illusion.

Don't look outside yourself for validation. It can be a slippery slope or, like with Alice, a very deep hole! Instead, rely on your well-honed instincts as you go forward. A reminder: this isn't your first experience when it comes to taking your power and getting things done. Trust that you know who you are and what you're doing. Say that again: "I trust who I am and what I'm doing."

EIGHT of WANDS

KEYWORDS

Swiftness, momentum, communication, expansion, vision, opportunity, inclusiveness

RULER: Mercury in Sagittarius

Ruled by Sagittarius, the sign of the Archer, the Eight of Wands says it's time to shoot your "arrows" into the world and get your ideas out there. You don't know where they will land, but what's important is that you actively share your inspirations. The *Couture*'s Eight of Wands offers a fashionable twist on traditional versions of this card. Instead of wands or batons flying through the air—we have shoes! Shoes or wands, they indicate a powerful trajectory of forward movement. There can be a bit of "What the hell—I'm just gonna do this," and that's right! I often describe this card as "throwing spaghetti against the wall and seeing what sticks." Do not hesitate. This is a sign to get out there.

This card reminds us that self-expression comes in an array of colors. Just think how boring life would be if we were all the same! Let go of past misunderstandings and see your way into a bigger picture—one that is inclusive and universal. Then, grab on to the great momentum offered here and communicate your vision with vigor!

NINE of WANDS

KEYWORDS

Strength, wholeness, protection, realization, purpose, integration, new consciousness

RULER: Sun in Sagittarius

A journey of self-discovery is reaching completion, and you are readying yourself for what is next. You are on the cusp of a new consciousness, and it is beginning to take tangible form. There are a lot of layers to the Nine of Wands, in the best sense. I chose to use a bust of a philosopher, an archetype of the deep thinker, a person who seeks wisdom or enlightenment, to center the card. This is a moment to integrate your journey thus far from a bigger (or higher) perspective. In a sense—reach for the stars! One of my favorite elements of this card is the expanse of dark skies above, filled with stars. Finally, in the background are walls of stones and flowers, indicating protection.

Old wounds may resurface as a part of integrating the past. Your new sense of wholeness is powerful, but it also brings to light those situations and relationships that are not in alignment with your greater evolution. Ask yourself: Is this a time to "forgive and forget"? You may feel protective of your space. Honor this. The old and familiar no longer serves, and you are reconfiguring what this means to you.

TEN of WANDS

KEYWORDS

Oppression, heaviness, isolation, burdens, obstacles, freedom, rebirth

RULER: Saturn in Sagittarius

The number ten represents completion. Yet, the Ten of Wands indicates that you are carrying the past forward, feeling like you need to keep working toward some outlived goal. In a word: Baggage! Hence the designer suitcases stacked upon each other. If there was ever a time for a purge, an emotional closet cleaning, this is it. Consider whether you are taking on too much responsibility for others. You have the right to act on your own inspirations and impulses. This is not being selfish. Dare to put your needs ahead of others.

Holding on to the past is a burden and ultimately becomes an obstacle to welcoming the new. The end result is blocked and stagnant energies—emotionally, creatively, spiritually—which can lead to depression, or anger. Your spirit is too big to be repressed; it seeks freedom. If there is anything you need to bring to completion, do so with integrity, consciously making amends as needed. Then let go and be at peace. Rebirth awaits!

PAGE *of* WANDS

KEYWORDS

Creativity, beginnings, adventure, play, self-expression, exploration, fearlessness

RULER: The Season of Spring

The Page of Wands is ready for adventure! Her staff (or wand) has just begun to sprout. She carries the energy of spring, a time of growth and the blossoming of new potentials. The Page of Wands shouts: INDIVIDUALITY! Whether it's her wild outfit, bright-orange hair and tribal makeup, or just general attitude, it's pretty obvious this Page has no desire to "fit in." They are who they are, a celebration of creativity. The orange fruit represents the juicy sweetness of spring. The butterfly on her sneakers indicates she has plenty of momentum on her journey.

The Page of Wands' playground is a fertile one, filled with learning experiences and growth. The future is not her concern, nor are outcomes. She would rather play in the potential of what is now. The Page of Wands indicates that you are being freed to explore your life in new and exciting ways. She encourages you to be brave and not give in to old fears. Let her vibrant energy guide you to fully inhabiting this moment.

KNIGHT of WANDS

KEYWORDS

Seeker, adventurous, energetic, rebellious, individualistic, growth oriented, creative spirit

RULER: Leo

The Knight of Wands is a fiery hunter, seeking avenues to break free of establishment in order to prove and define himself. The *Couture*'s Knight of Wands mirrors a dashing, Victorian-era hero, with one eye to the future and one eye to the past. The Victorian era was a time of sweeping progress, new discoveries, and ingenuity. His cape is made of butterfly wings, giving him the appearance of flight and the promise of freedom. A rare and endangered white crane elegantly folds into the Knight. In Chinese mythology, the crane represents immortality.

The Knight of Wands is tired of the old, staid ways of society and is daring to forge his own path. His bold moves may test others. He has little time for anyone else's needs other than his own, but his self-involvement is all in the name of self-discovery! Ambitious and rebellious, this Knight sees every challenge as an opportunity to more fully express his individuality. He is a testament to the creative spirit that seeks freedom and lies within us all!

QUEEN *of* WANDS

KEYWORDS

Wisdom, compassion, inspiration, transformation, intuition, bravery, self-realization

RULER: Aries

The Queen of Wands is sometimes referred to as the "Queen of Wisdom." Yet, her wisdom does not come from a book; instead it comes from her own life journey. She has experienced the often-difficult road toward self-realization. In the process she has transformed herself and now sees life through a radiant, multicolored lens.

When the mystic Gerd Ziegler talked about the Queen of Wands, he said, "The story says that she at one time had black hair, and the black panther was her companion. As she transformed, her hair turned to golden blond, and the panther became a lion. However, her desire to help others led her to choose to wear reddish-blond hair and make the leopard her companion. The Leopard's black spots became a reminder of her dark past, a powerful emblem to all overcoming their own struggles."

The Queen of Wands encourages you to fully embrace your life experience! It is who you are, and that experience is very powerful. Grab ahold of the inspiration coming your way and make it your own. Whenever possible, share your story with others. Your journey could be a motivational light for people as they overcome their own struggles.

KING of WANDS

KEYWORDS

Creative, charismatic, worldly wise, courageous, life affirming, self-centeredness, self-mastery

RULER: Sagittarius

The King of Wands is the most charismatic of all the Tarot's Kings! He is the one that everyone invites to the party because they want what he has—a life rich with experience. The *Couture*'s King of Wands is a bon vivant: dapper of dress, feather in his crown. He is surrounded by beautiful art (surely a collector!) and the effects of his many travels. Even though you can't see it, there's a rousing cocktail party going on in the background. He is also a tiger, the animal totem representing strength, confidence, and power.

The King of Wands is highly creative, not only in an artistic sense but also in creating a life filled with adventures and growth opportunities. At times he is worldly, debonair, and talented; yet, at other times, he can be egotistical and self-centered. The King of Wands signals a time to boldly become your passions. He indicates self-mastery, which comes from knowing who you are and standing for it. The more you fully inhabit the authentic you, the more opportunities will come.

THE SUIT OF CUPS:
WATER

In the Tarot's Cups, we dive into the inner mystery, the watery depths of your psyche: feelings and emotions, illusion and imagination, intuition and soul connections. Cups are the feminine/yin, soulful, receiving counterpart to the more aggressive, forward-moving, masculine/yang energies of the suit of Wands. Cups explore what's going on in your inner world, and their messages are often promptings from your unconscious/subconscious. As mentioned, they are associated with the suit of Hearts in traditional playing cards and ultimately lead you to discoveries of love: universally, within yourself, and with others.

ACE of CUPS

KEYWORDS

Beginnings, love, emotional purity, intuition, soul awakening, giving and receiving, universal flow

RULER: The element of Water

The Ace of Cups promises new beginnings, emotionally, in love, and within the deepest levels of your being. It represents a spiritual rebirth—an awakening!—of your soul. Look closely. In the background you can see a winking eye and what looks to be several small angels: one on the eyelid and one underneath. When I created this card, I did not purposely choose those images. I was just making a background. It was when the card was scanned that I saw the eye and angels, giving me the feeling of being divinely guided. This Ace opens your heart to greater potentials and heightens your gift of intuition. This is a time to trust your feelings and impressions, knowing that they are in alignment with your soul.

The watery energy of the Ace of Cups connects you to a universal flow of giving and receiving. Inspiration and ideas flourish as you experience a sense of divine abundance—one based in love and compassion. Give your imagination free rein to explore. The possibilities are endless.

TWO of CUPS

KEYWORDS

Happiness, romance, love, union, attraction, soul connections, blessings

RULER: Venus in Cancer

The Two of Cups indicates that your heart is open to deep and rewarding emotional exchanges; a giving and receiving of love in equal measure. Pictured are two lovebirds. Will they take the plunge into the "birdbath" below (Hello, Ultimate Kiss shower curtain!)? I hope so. It is rare when you find another whom you feel you can share your deepest self with, honestly, openly, and without artifice. This is a blessing and a gift. Your willingness to receive this gift is what attracts love to you.

I often call the Two of Cups the "soulmate" card, because no matter the outcome, there can be a feeling of profound recognition, déjà vu, an eternal connectiveness. Don't worry that this is too good to be true; you would only be doubting yourself. No one knows what the future holds, so for now, enjoy this moment and bathe in the love coming to you.

THREE of CUPS

KEYWORDS

Emotional abundance, love, nurturance, friendship, celebration, communication, enjoyment

RULER: Mercury in Cancer

The Three of Cups is an emotionally abundant card. Here, the gifts of the heart are rich and plentiful and should be nurtured with the utmost care. This card encourages you to fully enjoy your relationships and friendships, especially since there is a new harmony present. I come from a family of three sisters. For the *Couture*'s Three of Cups, I envisioned us as three beautifully coiffed pink flamingos coming together for afternoon tea. We are dressed accordingly: hats, flower boas, neckwear, and earrings. Me? I'm the middle one. The creative flamingo. I smile every time I see this card. It fills my heart with joy, which is its very essence.

This is a time to freely communicate your feelings as a way of inviting more intimacy. If you have been holding back on sharing your heart with someone, now is the time! Your love is pure and true, and no matter the outcome it is a gift that needs to be shared and celebrated. This is a sweet communion—enjoy it!

FOUR of CUPS

KEYWORDS

Reflection, inner communion, feelings, sensitivity, luxury, tenderness, self-care

RULER: Moon in Cancer

This card carries a strong lunar influence. Just as the moon has her cycles, your emotional tides have their ebb and flow. The Four of Cups represents an inward cycle; a time to go within to reflect on your emotional journey. Instead of taking care of others, this is a time to take care of *you*. In the process, it is important to be gentle and tender with yourself. You're feeling sensitive, and your message to others is "Tread lightly." Your proverbial cups are dry, and you need to refill them.

In numerology, the number four represents stability, foundations, and rest. For now, you don't need to figure it all out. There's no rush, and you'll know when you're ready. Embrace the luxury of taking time to commune and nurture your deepest self. This is rich territory, and the right attitude will bring you peace of mind and heart. You deserve it.

FIVE of CUPS

KEYWORDS

Change, disappointment, grief, sentimentality, emotional loss, release, healing

RULER: Mars in Scorpio

The number five carries the vibration of change. When combined with the watery-feeling orientation of the suit of Cups, it can be experienced as emotional loss. The *Couture*'s Five of Cups is set in a Parisian, sepia-toned landscape. Its essence reminds me of the movie *Casablanca*, at the end, when Rick is sending Elsa away. "We'll always have Paris," he says. The sorrowful poignancy of that moment feels very Five of Cups. The old image of the three ladies is from the 1920s, and the lavender—a flower known for grace and healing.

Keep in mind that change—and its shadow, loss—is a part of the continuum of life. Don't let disappointments keep you from embracing the emotional release and letting go that needs to happen. Sentimentality and nostalgia can inhibit you from moving forward. If you're looking backward, your journey ahead will be fraught with confusion. The Five of Cups, more than anything else, is about taking time to grieve what is lost. Once you do so, you will experience a profound emotional healing, leading to a new sense of clarity.

SIX of CUPS

KEYWORDS

Emotional renewal, deep bonds, pleasure, nostalgia, intimacy, memories, transformation

RULER: Sun in Scorpio

Like a phoenix rising from the ashes, this card indicates transformation, an emotional renewal. You are ready to breathe new life into your relationships—both old and new. There is a wispy, dreamy vibe to this card. A sweetness. This is a time when memories may resurface, bringing new clarity and understanding to your journey. You may experience full-circle moments, helping you integrate the past and move forward with a new sense of wholeness.

In the background we see an angel lifted by an ashen phoenix, old-time lovers at the end of a long path, and two turtle doves.

The Six of Cups encourages you to partake in the pleasures of intimacy as you recognize deep emotional bonds. Old lovers and friends may "unexpectedly" show up in your life. Embrace the happiness and healing these relationships can bring. There is great richness here. In the best sense, everything old is new again.

SEVEN of CUPS

KEYWORDS

Unbalanced emotions, desire, illusion, debauchery, shadow side, deception, power

RULER: Venus in Scorpio

The Seven of Cups is tricky terrain, as you negotiate confusing feelings and wants. This card is sometimes portrayed as the Seven Deadly Sins (pride, greed, wrath, envy, lust, gluttony, sloth), alluding to the trappings of false desires. When you are out of balance emotionally, your unfulfilled longings may not be coming from a healthy place. This is a time to look at whether whom or what you are lusting for is real and valuable, or an illusion, what could be described as a projection of your shadow side.

Our shadow represents parts of ourselves we hide away because it makes us uncomfortable. Like a snake in the grass waiting to strike, it will, often appearing through the veil of unrealized desires. If not addressed, your shadow's mischief can become dangerous to your well-being. Your heart knows what is true and will mediate between what is real and what is not. Know that true desire does not deceive. See through the illusion and take your power back.

EIGHT of CUPS

KEYWORDS

Stagnation, emotional blockage, darkness, healing, regret, hardship, release

RULER: Saturn in Pisces

The Eight of Cups is sometimes acquainted with the "Dark Night of the Soul." The Soul's Dark Night is described as a spiritual and existential crisis. It may be painful, but it is ultimately transformative. This card warns of getting caught up in bitterness or disappointments about "what might have been." Your regrets can become an endless compulsion. The perched Owl is a welcome beacon in this dark night. It is a reminder of the great wisdom and transformation that comes only from going into the darkness. The time has come to recognize unfulfilling relationships that are draining you. It takes strength to no longer participate in soul-depleting situations.

With this card there can be the experience of weariness, a feeling of emotional and spiritual exhaustion. Life has become a burden, leading to stagnation, even hopelessness. Like a record player with your needle stuck in an old groove, you may find yourself going round and round. Use the wisdom of your past experiences, set new boundaries, and move forward.

NINE of CUPS

NINE of CUPS

KEYWORDS

Deep joy, happiness, blessings, purification, emotional fulfillment, gratitude, overflowing love

RULER: Jupiter in Pisces

This card indicates that your proverbial cups are full and you now have the energy to focus on the things you love. I call this card "swimming with happiness!" Hence the lovely bathing beauties. There is a sensation of emotional abundance—each new day becomes a blessing in itself. The overall feeling is that of gratitude for the gifts you have received. Some refer to the Nine of Cups as "wishes fulfilled." This happiness is not an illusion. It is deeply rooted in the waters of your soul, the essence of your being.

If you're not yet in the "swim," reflect on whether you feel you deserve to receive happiness. This is a time to forgive yourself or others, so you can fully experience the joy coming to you. Reward yourself by doing something special. Sometimes, you just need to get out of your own way and receive the gifts of joy waiting for you.

TEN of CUPS

KEYWORDS

Emotional satiety, serenity, fulfillment, peace, enjoyment, receiving, completion

RULER: Mars in Pisces

The Ten of Cups indicates a time when your emotional waters still. There is a beautiful peace this card brings, since you no longer need to engage in the drama of unfulfilled desires. You feel secure within yourself and have everything you need. I often describe this card as "coming home to self." This sense of inner security is a powerful foundation for whatever comes next. The rest, as they say, is the icing on the cake!

Ten is the number of completion, and in the Ten of Cups you fully realize an emotional cycle with your family, relationships, and your literal sense of home. For now, the work is done and you are free to savor the moment before moving forward. Let things develop on their own. You might even find that opportunities come to you without having to work for them. The Ten of Cups also holds the possibility for bringing some long-held dreams into fruition—like visiting your favorite escape or ticking something off your bucket list. At the end of this chapter, it's important to take time and enjoy what you have created. Breathe deeply and fully receive this moment.

PAGE *of* CUPS

KEYWORDS

Emotional freedom, heart openings, grace, innocence, vulnerability, playfulness, new love

RULER: The Season of Summer

In the *Couture Tarot*, the Page of Cups is a mermaid gracefully rising from the depths of a magical sea. Her companion is a small sea turtle, signifying emotional strength and wisdom. She indicates a time when you are being freed from the tangled (sea) weeds of the past to venture forth. She wears a winged heart as a crest, showing both her vulnerability and her willingness to share her heart openly. This Page has no need for protection. Her innocence has become her strength, allowing her great emotional freedom.

One of the endearing qualities of the Tarot's Pages is their childlike sense of adventure and play. When this mermaid swims into your life, she is encouraging you to open your heart to new experiences. Frolic in the Sea of Love and explore its unlimited treasures and possibilities. It's time to play!

KNIGHT of CUPS

KEYWORDS

Love, longing, desire, romance, deep emotions, integrity, sexual energy, seduction

RULER: Scorpio

The Knight of Cups is a rogue pirate on a quest to fulfill his deepest longings. He indicates a time to look at your passions, desires, and sexual energies. Emotions run high while you learn to master your passions and live them with awareness. When out of balance, he can be a manipulator, seducing others to get his way. I created this Knight with the archetype of Lancelot, from the Arthurian legends, in mind. Lancelot, a true Knight of Hearts, fell in love with Arthur's bride, Guinevere, and ultimately his desire was his demise. He is a reminder that deception, even in the name of love, never wins.

With time, Lancelot became a crusader of the Holy Grail, representing eternal and unconditional love. This Knight also hints at transformation. By being willing to go into the crucible of your desires, you can find liberation. Free yourself from the hidden shadows and secrets that may bind you.

QUEEN of CUPS

KEYWORDS

Emotional confidence, nurturance, deep feelings, love, sensitivity, intuition, wisdom

RULER: Cancer

The Queen of Cups is surrounded by the waters of the sea, her natural domain. Symbolically, the realm of water carries many moods and emotions, waves of deeper thoughts and feelings. The Queen of Cups has learned to be at peace with the natural flow of life's currents. She wears a pearl as an earring, showing her connection to the sea and its timeless wisdom. If you're looking for comfort, this nurturing Queen will provide a safe harbor. She is confident in her feelings and emotions, knowing that her sensitivity—the ability to feel profoundly—is integral to her power.

The Queen of Cups can be a mysterious presence, one that is not always understood intellectually. Truly understanding her and her exquisitely changing moods will come only with trust. This is a time to allow your intuition to flow, and to be secure in your sense of knowing. You have a deep mystery that others can only begin to perceive. Love emanates as you give others a glimpse into your soul.

KING of CUPS

KEYWORDS

Emotional mastery, integrity, intimacy, heart connections, empathy, enriching relationships, fulfillment

RULER: Pisces

The King of Cups is a Captain of Hearts. He has sailed the emotional seas and weathered many storms to become a wise and empathic King. He represents a time for deepening your relationships—with romantic partners, and within both your birth and spiritual family. Having the inner security to share your emotions openly and with integrity invites more intimacy into your life.

This card is special to me. I modeled it after my father, a man who cherished his time in the US Navy. A water sign—Scorpio—of another generation (he was born during the Depression), he wasn't the easiest of men or fathers. Yet, at the time that he passed on, we had come to a loving reckoning, and I miss him daily. This King has learned the difference between fantasy and imagined longings, and what is real and possible. This is emotional mastery! Trust your heart, let go of ambivalence, and fully embrace the love present in your life.

THE SUIT OF SWORDS:
AIR

In the suit of Swords, we engage the element of Air, representing the mind, intellect, inspiration, knowledge, and wisdom. Whereas the previous suit of Cups is about feelings and emotions, Swords are about information and facts. The Swords cards often indicate your analytical mind and thought process: "I think, therefore I am." Swords offer perception and wisdom, encouraging you to consciously discern the facts and come to your own understanding. This suit is associated with the principle of truth, the search for higher meaning to your existence and mundane reality.

ACE of SWORDS

KEYWORDS

Clarity, brilliance, divine truth, power, integrity, will, destiny

RULER: The element of Air

Throughout the ages, the sword has been a symbol of rulership and divine truth. It represents the spiritual will that conquers fear and self-doubt through the strength of clear thinking. The sword is also known as the force of intuition, the higher mind. Think of mythology's young King Arthur, who drew the sword Excalibur from the stone and took his rightful place of power. According to legend, when a person holds the magic sword, they are mentally empowered, allowing them to follow their path of destiny.

The *Couture*'s Ace of Swords is a diamond ring. The diamond is able to cut through most substances and is known for its clarity and integrity. This card calls you to *your* destiny—now is the time to seize your power! Your determination brings the might of your mind and will toward manifestation. It is this singular focus that achieves great things. The Ace of Swords has the potential to clear away negative thinking and bring profound clarity and realization.

TWO of SWORDS

KEYWORDS

Peace, intuition, balance, centeredness, friendship, decisions, serenity

RULER: Moon in Libra

The *Couture*'s Two of Swords shows two dogs sitting on opposite sides of a church; the church is a traditional symbol for safety and sanctuary. One dog wears a silver crown, the other gold. Behind them is a bleak, gray landscape, indicating that situations haven't been unfolding in a harmonious manner. The Two of Swords calls you to "lay down your sword," to surrender the conflicts and discord in your life and be at peace. Essentially, time for a détente.

This card often shows up when you are struggling with a decision. Your mind is saying one thing, and your heart another. The Two of Swords encourages you to find a balance between the two. When your mind and heart come together in friendship, a powerful alchemy occurs. The result is profound balance. The way you engage this alchemy is by listening to your intuition. This is the voice of a mindful heart. Doing so will bring new clarity and a welcomed sense of serenity.

THREE *of* SWORDS

KEYWORDS

Truth, authenticity, heartbreak, disappointment, justice, liberation, piercing through illusion

RULER: Saturn in Libra

Traditionally the Three of Swords shows a big red heart pierced by three swords. In the *Couture Tarot*, the image becomes a piercing, red stiletto boot. Either way, there is a piercing, a cutting away. This cutting away is usually around a relationship or a matter of the heart. In the simplest of terms, and whatever the situation, this card represents heartbreak. Often there is a decision that must be made, and putting off that decision will only delay the pain. You cannot avoid the truth that is before you. Although it can be painful, this card brings liberation as you see through illusion to find the truth.

Don't get stuck in the disappointment of what might have been. Instead embrace the silver lining presented in the Three of Swords—the opportunity to live a more authentic life. There is a "lesson learned" aspect to this card, potentially moving you forward in new ways. Stand in your clarity and trust that spiritual justice and healing will come. The heart seeks integrity, and Divine Truth always prevails.

FOUR of SWORDS

KEYWORDS

Truce, calm, recharge, serenity, centeredness, integration, renewal

RULER: Jupiter in Libra

The Four of Swords indicates a truce. This could come in the form of a new understanding between you and another, an intentional respite from a challenging situation, or simply embracing a renewed sense of serenity within. In the best sense, you've "read the room" and know that it's time to step back. You do not need to figure anything out; instead, allow the forces at play to naturally find their way to a favorable solution. The *Couture*'s Four of Swords shows a Sleeping Beauty atop a bed of tulips. "Rest, my sweet," the image says. "Rest."

The Four of Swords is a time of integration. This comes from letting go so that a healthful renewal can take place. This is a stepback, not a set back; it is necessary to the creative process. Whenever possible, extend the olive branch of peace to others. You may be surprised at how this gesture is reciprocated, bringing more harmony into your life. Peace begets peace. Grace begets grace.

FIVE of SWORDS

KEYWORDS

Mental chaos, worry, fear, anguish, defeatism, patience, surrender

RULER: Venus in Aquarius

The Five of Swords indicates that you are overthinking aspects of your life, to the point of losing any true sense of clarity. The five eyes on this card represent the ruminating you may be doing, and that, no matter how you look at it—up, down, right, or left—you can't think yourself out of this situation! Your mind is too powerful to waste on indecision or defeating thoughts. This will only cause pointless anguish. Especially when the situation you are focused on is probably influx, with the outcome to be determined. What you are likely experiencing now is fear; namely, the general feeling of being out of control.

Time to step back and view things from a greater perspective. Just imagine how wonderful your life could be if you were not afraid of failure! Although you may want to figure everything out as soon as possible, this is not the moment. Know that you will have more clarity when the dust settles. In the meantime, refocus your energies on what you love to do, and, from there, what you need will come.

SIX of SWORDS

KEYWORDS

Perspective, vision, movement, ease, grace, understanding, objectivity

RULER: Mercury in Aquarius

The Six of Swords offers perspective as you integrate your past experiences and begin to view them objectively. Insight and revelation take the place of worry and doubt, presenting a new vision for traveling forward. Indeed, the Six of Swords can represent travel—in this case, a long-awaited voyage, away from the difficulties of the past. Our Six of Swords shows a green velvet couch—the *Couture*'s version of a boat—floating across fields of flowers. The boat is guided by a hawk, taking the place of the traditional boatman usually presented. The hawk/boatman is integral, since it is their presence that reminds you that now you don't have to do everything alone.

Be open to messages—from others, the world, and divine forces—as guidance. Then, as you feel ready, express your ideas with others. Allow yourself to ease into a new flow, since you no longer need to swim upstream. This is a time to move forward with confidence and assurance. This card carries a graceful spirit, one that allows a gentle emergence into a world of possibilities.

SEVEN of SWORDS

SEVEN of SWORDS

KEYWORDS

Illusion, deception, futility, negative expectations, imagination, discernment, awareness

RULER: Moon in Aquarius

The Seven of Swords encourages a reality check, since wishful thinking may be clouding your vision. The imagination is a wondrous and powerful force, but it may be deceiving you now. Without awareness, your hope for greater things can lead you down a dark rabbit hole of misperception and confusion. The *Couture*'s Seven of Swords shows an Alice in Wonderland type of figure, along with the white rabbit to emphasize this point. Too many distractions are drawing your attention away from a clear path. As a result, you may feel lost, experiencing fear and anxiety—even futility.

This is a time to be careful about your boundaries, especially around the expectations of others. Look behind the masks of projection and illusion and stay true to you. Nurture your dreams with the attention they deserve, while also staying grounded. Set aside negative thinking and focus your attention on the present moment. This will help you discern what is real and what is not. Then you can open yourself to real and life-affirming possibilities.

EIGHT of SWORDS

KEYWORDS

Stress, overthinking, mental endurance, interference, decisions, discovery, big picture

RULER: Jupiter in Gemini

The Eight of Swords often appears when you are trying to make decisions about your future. You are attempting to connect all the dots and come up with a logical course of action. Yet, the harder you try to find solutions, the more you become tangled in a maze of your thoughts. The Eight of Swords is an indication that you do not have the clarity at this time to find satisfactory answers. I often call this card "becoming a prisoner of one's own mind." Or, in other words, you're overthinking things!

Time to step back and allow solutions to show themselves. You are in a process of discovery, and the facts are not in place to make clear decisions. This may test your patience and endurance. You will need to think long term versus short term. Keep the big picture in mind and don't rush toward quick solutions. The Eight of Swords can also be a harbinger of change and unexpected outcomes for the better. Now more than ever, this is a time to surrender your intellectual mind and thought process to something greater.

NINE of SWORDS

KEYWORDS

Mental pollution, punishment, martyrdom, helplessness, fear, consciousness, self-love

RULER: Mars in Gemini

The Nine of Swords represents a mental dead end. A time when your thought process is so polluted by fear and negative thinking that your mind basically implodes. Nothing good comes from this state of being, and your mental health is at stake. If something or someone is endangering your inner peace, it's time to move on. Consider if you have become stuck in a punishing thought process that has become a habit. This only reinforces your fears and limits your ability to see clearly.

The way to clear this "mind smog" is to take back your power by remembering that you are greater than your thoughts. When in balance, our thinking minds are essential to our life process. When out of balance, they push away our intuition, creativity, and self-trust. Don't be hard on yourself; shift your consciousness toward self-love. As you say "no" to mental cruelty, you will experience a peace of mind that is rejuvenating and powerful!

TEN *of* SWORDS

KEYWORDS

Destruction, betrayal, clarity, vision, transformation, truth, illumination

RULER: Sun and Moon in Gemini

The traditional Ten of Swords often shows a man betrayed, pierced in the back by ten swords. In the *Couture*'s Ten of Swords, we see something completely different: a crystal staircase guarded by an angelic presence. In creating the deck, I felt that it was important to reimagine this card, to take it out of the old-school macabre visual that is normally portrayed and to offer a different take.

Indeed, the Ten of Swords represents endings, which can certainly be painful. There is often a reckoning, a realization, a need to see the truth. But instead of just suffering through the experience, embrace the opportunity to rise above your mental fears and find ultimate clarity. Situations that do not serve your highest potential are coming to an end. Consider this the death of old ways of thinking and being; rebirth and transformation await! This is a time to elevate your thought process by seeing life through the crystal-clear lens of what is real. Your truth is being illuminated. Reach for the light.

PAGE of SWORDS

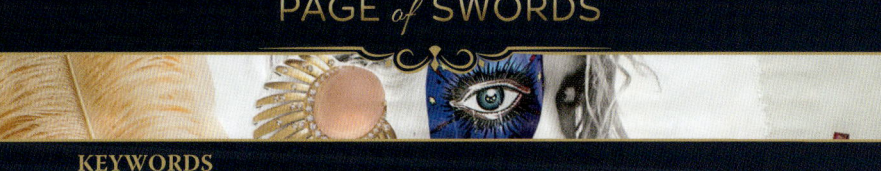

KEYWORDS

Change, breakthroughs, ideas, communication, mental liberation, curiosity, rebellion

RULER: The Season of Autumn

The Page of Swords is a messenger of change. She represents a fresh perspective; an awakening to new and different possibilities. Once embraced, her view is so compelling that it inspires rebellious and independent thinking. This ever-curious Page is ready to shake things up and explore new ideas! A great communicator, she is able to expound on many different concepts at the same time.

This Page signals a time when you are breaking free of old limitations, especially intellectually and how you view the world. You no longer have patience for the banal and uninspiring. The winds of change have begun to blow, and you're filled with new ideas. Communication is key now. Do not hesitate to share your thoughts and ideas with others. If they get it—great! If not, you may be ahead of your time. Like a doubled-edged sword, the Page of Swords can be brash, outspoken, and arrogant but also carries a youthful energy and the innocence to believe in greater possibilities.

KNIGHT of SWORDS

KEYWORDS

Creative thinking, discovery, innovation, inspiration, higher concepts, ingenuity, reinvention

RULER: Aquarius

Like all Knights of the Tarot, the Knight of Swords is a seeker. In his case, searching for new avenues of mental and intellectual discovery. He has learned the great power of the mind and is looking for opportunities to channel it in new ways. The Knight of Swords is both scientist and metaphysician, and like many innovators before him, he seeks to reconfigure old theories and concepts. He is not bound by rules or convention, but instead he is finding his own way.

I imagined the Knight of Swords as the essence of Pythagoras, combined with Leonardo da Vinci, and some Nikola Tesla thrown in! What these luminaries have in common is the genius to think outside the box—to aspire to bigger concepts about how the universe works. When this inventive Knight rides into your life, it is a time to listen to your inspirations and channel your own ingenuity into new ways of thinking and being. Genius aside, the Knight of Swords can be hard to pin down and elusive in relationships, since they tend to live more in their mind than in their hearts.

QUEEN of SWORDS

KEYWORDS

Logic, truth, arbitration, justice, objectivity, insight, balance

RULER: Libra

The Queen of Swords is the master of her domain, the realm of Air. Air symbolizes the intellect, ideas, and critical thought. She is not the warmest of Queens; in fact, some may call her cold. The Queen of Swords rules from her mind, not her emotions. For this critical Queen, there are no gray areas—her viewpoint is often black and white, with little room for nuances. Hers is a double-edged sword, the ability to see both sides of the situation. She can represent your inner critic, the desire to make everything right and perfect. Yet, she is a great arbitrator of truth and fairness and brings a rational clarity to most situations.

The Queen of Swords encourages you to be objective in your dealings with others and not give in to irrational thinking. She offers the gift of clarity, which comes from a strong moral compass and a detachment from the opinions of others. This Queen brings the ability to balance judgmental thinking with the highest good.

KING of SWORDS

KEYWORDS

Wisdom, clarity, noble intentions, discernment, truth, intellect, intuition

RULER: Gemini

This King of Swords comes in the form of an owl, the animal totem representing wisdom and the ability to see through illusion to find the truth. He indicates a time when your intellectual prowess is heightened, with a desire to master new forms of knowledge. Wisdom is more than knowledge, however. It comes from the ability to examine the facts and come to an expanded understanding. In the best sense, this King understands how to balance his intuition—his deeper knowing—with his intellect. The King of Swords offers perspective and clarity to your journey.

This is a great time to look to the future, since there is momentum for establishing new plans. This may come in the form of writing, design, architecture, or academic pursuits. Much like a journalist, you may feel a passion to share the facts with others—all in service of the truth. The King of Swords wears a bee talisman. The bee represents innovation, wisdom, and community. Let this wise and noble mentor guide you to mastering your real truth.

THE SUIT OF PENTACLES
EARTH

Pentacles represent the realm of Earth, rooting us in our physical and material natures. Pentacles ground us in the real world, bringing manifestation and the fulfillment of goals. In some decks, Pentacles are called Coins, pertaining to abundance: money, security, and what makes you thrive. Pentacles also relate to physical health and well-being. They are the final suit of the Minor Arcana, an accumulation of the previous suits, as we realize our earthly journey. These cards represent the soul embodied, the pleasure of fully engaging in physical existence. Here we reap what we sow.

ACE of PENTACLES

KEYWORDS

Abundance, initiation, consciousness, manifestation, grounding, celebration, body and soul

RULER: The element of Earth

The Ace of Pentacles represents new opportunities in the physical and material world. It symbolizes the gift of life and its inherent riches. Embrace the heaven-sent ability to manifest the abundant reality you have always wished for. In this card, body meets soul—or, as the mystics say, "as above, so below." The Ace of Pentacles represents a shift in consciousness and the realization that your body is the vehicle for your divine self.

The deeper you connect within your body, the more your soul has wings to soar! This is a time to take good care of yourself, especially your health. You are the vessel for your newfound abundance and prosperity. By celebrating each moment, you anchor yourself in the here and now, which is where all creation begins. Take time to root into Mother Earth and then enjoy the many vicissitudes of life. This is a fresh start.

TWO of PENTACLES

KEYWORDS

Change, balance, transformation, harmony, opportunity, financial management, alignment

RULER: Jupiter in Capricorn

The Two of Pentacles is a sign of changing energy, especially of a financial nature. The number two represents balance, and the Two of Pentacles indicates that you are looking for more harmony in your material world. This is a time to reevaluate your monies and make sure they are allocated toward bringing you security. Be open to making changes to bring your affairs into order.

Although the Two of Pentacles deals with the mundane, material realm, it also has a "higher" aspect: it carries an uplifting potential—a greater flow between your higher self and actualization. When your needs and wants are in alignment, the possibilities for abundance are endless. This is a time to embrace change, because that's where your best opportunities lie. At the same time, it's important not to go to extremes in the process. Balance and integrity are key now to future success.

THREE *of* PENTACLES

KEYWORDS

Work, diligence, future-building, mastery, gradual process, collaboration, craftsmanship

RULER: Mars in Capricorn

The Three of Pentacles indicates a stage of work, knowing that the time now spent honing your craft will lead to future success. Diligence is key, as is a patient attitude. With creating any masterpiece, it starts with chisel to stone, pen to paper, and love, sweat, and tears! You are feeling passionate about your work; yet, on this path you may also feel vulnerable or doubtful of your abilities. Remember, you are in a process of developing your skills. You are more student here than teacher, but no lesser because so.

You may find it useful to create in a collaborative setting. Be open to working with others, especially those who can help you grow your talents. Take advantage of opportunities for internships or apprenticeships. Lean into this exceptionally creative period. Do not put pressure on yourself or look for perfection. For now, it's all about the learning, the crafting, and the growth.

FOUR of PENTACLES

KEYWORDS

Security, financial stability, investment, reliability, foundations, conservative, integrity

RULER: Sun in Capricorn

The Four of Pentacles represents stability for your finances and for life in general. It indicates that you have built solid and reliable foundations that will serve you well. Although it may be your instinct to advance your undertakings, now is not the time. Instead, enjoy the security that you have created. This is a time to be conservative in your actions and reinvest in your current situation. For now, saying "no" is likely your best bet. It may seem as if you're playing it safe, but what you are actually doing is giving yourself the time to shore up and strengthen your financial boundaries.

This card emphasizes integrity—within yourself and your monies. If there's anything that needs to be resolved, this is the moment. You will find that being on top of your current situation brings power to what you manifest next. For now, save your coins for another day.

FIVE of PENTACLES

KEYWORDS

Fortune, change, loss, pessimism, idleness, poverty mentality, new perspective

RULER: Mercury in Taurus

The Five of Pentacles points to a fragile moment, since you are on the cusp of change. It could feel like the very ground beneath you is falling away, and that good fortune is unattainable. As hard as it may be, you need to allow for some things to go to make way for new abundance. The Five of Coins is a notoriously "negative" card, because it speaks to potential loss. Yet, if you quiet your fear, you can begin to see the hidden potential that is all around you. Open your mind to the infinite possibilities that come from releasing old, blocked energy and embracing change.

Be careful about getting caught in a victim- or poverty-based mentality. Don't let pessimism keep you idle; instead gather yourself and bring your attention to practical matters. A hopeful perspective could tip the balance. When the Universe closes a door, it also opens a window. You are an abundant manifestation just waiting to happen!

SIX of PENTACLES

KEYWORDS

Success, abundance, harmony, giving and receiving, goodwill, generosity, gratitude

RULER: Moon in Taurus

The Six of Pentacles is a gift; one of your own making, although it may seem like a miracle bestowed. This card indicates that you are experiencing greater personal and financial success. It is a sign to stay true to your efforts and that you are on track to realize your goals. As you embrace abundance, you are compelled to share it with others. Like the figure shown, you are inspired to give and encourage others to do the same. This card brings out your benevolent nature, calling you to become a generous patron within your community.

The Six of Pentacles is a reminder of the power of kindness. The idea that the more you give, the more you receive. But don't forget the receiving! Being open and available to others' generosity, whatever the form, is an important part of the equation. Sometimes the hardest action is to receive. Yet, it is important to the flow of abundance. Embrace the harmony that is present with a grateful heart.

SEVEN of PENTACLES

KEYWORDS

Fear of failure, obstacles, overwork, patience, persistence, nurturance, long-term success

RULER: Saturn in Taurus

The Seven of Pentacles appears when you are working toward a goal, but it hasn't become fully realized. Your first instinct might be to worry or try to remedy the situation. Well, Rome wasn't built in a day! It's not the destination, it's the journey. Savor the moment . . . don't give in to frustration. Resist overworking the situation or holding on too tightly. Remember, negative expectations only muddy the process.

This is an active waiting period, as nature takes its course. The garden needs time to grow. In the process, you may need to do some weeding. If there are projects that don't have the potential to bear fruit, then it's time to let them go. Focus your energy on what can garner the most success. Find joy in what you are creating. This is powerful manna to fertilize your projects. Tomorrow is another day, and your blooms will be beautiful.

EIGHT *of* PENTACLES

KEYWORDS

Prudence, development, adjustment, carefulness, endurance, satisfaction, hard work

RULER: Sun in Virgo

The Eight of Pentacles represents a time when you are completing projects and making final adjustments to perfect your work. This may include securing aspects around money or business, or just being industrious in general. The Eight of Pentacles says that you are close to the finish line but may need to rally your efforts in order to complete the course. At the same time, this is not a moment to rush; you need to be careful with your craft. The Eight of Pentacles was partly inspired by the stamina of elk herds and the strength and resilience it takes to migrate over great distances.

There is power in what you're doing! Dig into the process and watch yourself grow and evolve. This will take endurance, so find satisfaction in the work. Your willingness to be in it for the long haul will bring future rewards. Like a fine whiskey, the ingredients to success take time to ferment.

NINE of PENTACLES

KEYWORDS

Gain, accomplishment, receiving, flowering, abundance, love, celebration

RULER: Venus in Virgo

In the Nine of Pentacles the fruits of your labor become apparent and fully realized. It is your unwavering devotion to the process that makes this moment possible. This card reinforces the idea that by loving what you do, the results will eventually come. Of course, the more you attend to and water those fruit, the lusher they will grow. Your success did not fall out of the sky; you created it and it should be celebrated—lavishly!

We all have unique talents and abilities, and it's important to take ownership of yours. Like a beautiful painting, we all are masterpieces in the making. There is a welcoming aspect to the Nine of Pentacles. The more you value your gifts and share them with others, the sweeter your abundance will be. This is a time to celebrate your accomplishments and appreciate the relationships that have gotten you here. Be present to this moment! You have earned it and need to fully take it in.

TEN of PENTACLES

KEYWORDS

Wealth, completion, security, satisfaction, reflection, enjoyment, letting go

RULER: Mercury in Virgo

The Ten of Pentacles is a time to come home to yourself and your accomplishments. Take satisfaction in work well done. This card indicates that you have completed a cycle, and now it's important to pause before a new season begins. Pentacles are associated with the winter season, ushering in a time of quiet reflection. The *Couture*'s Ten of Pentacles reminds me of Christmas (hence the gilded Christmas tree) and the magical wonders that take place at this time of year—a time when Santa Claus wishes come true, and your Christmas stockings are filled with treasure.

The Ten of Pentacles carries the spirit of abundance. This card is a reminder that prosperity comes in many forms, and some of our most abundant moments happen from simple pleasures. The gifts of spirit are rich and plentiful. Savor the security you are now experiencing. If there was a caution, it would only be not to become stagnant by holding on too tightly. By understanding that change is a part of life, you can more fully enjoy this precious time.

PAGE of PENTACLES

KEYWORDS

New possibilities, light, renewal, excitement, creativity, prolific, life affirming

RULER: The Season of Winter

The Page of Pentacles is like a ray of sunshine on a winter day! She indicates a time when the dark clouds part and you are ready to play with new possibilities. This Page carries a fertile energy and is often associated with the idea of birth, the bringing forth of new creations. The Page of Pentacles is exploring new expressions for herself in the material world, which may range from career and financial shifts to a new relationship with her body and wellness.

The Page of Pentacles brings a dynamic sense of excitement and adventure to your ventures. She represents the light of renewal, an infusion of spirit into matter. Dreams that have been in slumber can now take flight! When the Page of Pentacles comes your way, she indicates that you are looking for a fresh perspective around what you "do." Much like "What do I want to be when I grow up?" Time to play with all possibilities. Spirit is with you.

KNIGHT of PENTACLES

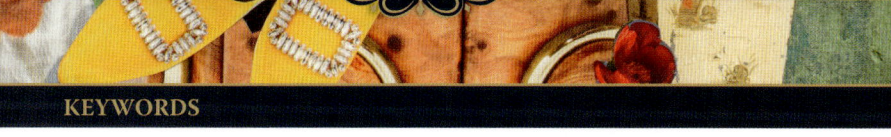

KEYWORDS

Perseverance, prudence, manifestation, stamina, goals, reliable and fulfilling work

RULER: Taurus

The Knight of Pentacles is known for his determination and unshakable perseverance. He is out to conquer the material world, and nothing will stop him from reaching his goals. Although ambitious, he is also prudent, knowing when to harness his energy so that he can successfully reach the finish line. He is someone you can rely on, especially when it comes to getting things done. I created the *Couture*'s Knight of Pentacles as a young, hardworking professional, coffee in hand and eager to show up and play the career game. He is similar in essence to the fable "The Tortoise and the Hare." We all know who made it to the finish line! With the Knight of Pentacles, slow and steady rules the day.

QUEEN of PENTACLES

KEYWORDS

Abundance, fruitfulness, nourishment, beauty, wholeness, rewards, actualization

RULER: Capricorn

The Queen of Pentacles is deeply rooted in the earth; she is a goddess reveling in her abundance. She is enjoying the fruits of her labor after the hard work it took to rise to her throne. She shows great beauty in her ascension. Like her talisman—the peacock—she represents the alchemy of actualization, the ability to transform toil into success and prosperity. Independent, tenacious, and kind, she is the model of "tough-love earth mother" and never hesitates to envelope you in her lush, nurturing folds.

When this Queen appears in your life, she is encouraging you to fully embody and take pride in what you have accomplished on a personal level—in relationships and family—and also around your career and the work you do. Like her counterpart, the King of Pentacles, she is on top of her professional game and is comfortable in her success. She indicates health and wealth, encouraging you to take time to enjoy life's richest rewards.

KING *of* PENTACLES

KEYWORDS

Success, power, investments, influence, stability, wealth, wisdom

RULER: Virgo

The King of Pentacles has mastered the material realm. He is a seasoned professional, having learned the rules of the game, elevating himself to the top of his field. He is the king of capital and has cemented his future investments. The *Couture*'s King of Pentacles is shown in a New York City landscape featuring the Empire State building, an icon of worldly commerce and power. As they say, "If you can make it in New York, you can make it anywhere!" This Earthly King indicates that you are on the path to fully embodying your potential in the "real" world.

He encourages you to wisely manage your wealth, both spiritually and materially. Although he sits alone, he knows the power of teamwork and is benevolent in nature. He takes great satisfaction in a robust, well-constructed life. Because he has achieved wealth and wisdom, he is a powerful role model for others. This King is a reminder that your success is more than just material goods—it also comes from living a holistic life.

COUTURE TAROT CARD SPREADS

In comparison to choosing a single card, a card spread can provide a more comprehensive understanding of a situation or aspect of your life. A spread is like a story unfolding, with the cards forming different relationships with one another.

Here are three card spreads created specifically for the *Couture Tarot*, along with a traditional Celtic Cross Spread. You can also make up your own layout, depending on the situation you wish to explore. Before doing a reading it is important to set the intention. This means taking a moment to become clear and centered, focusing on the matter you wish to be clarified.

THE DESTINY SPREAD

Soul
(PAST)

Spirit
(PRESENT)

Destiny
(FUTURE)

THE DESTINY SPREAD

1. Soul (Past): The inherent gifts that you were born with. It is your deepest self, incorporating memories, unconscious motivations, and the inner workings of your psyche. It may also represent the area where you get blocked or stuck in the comfort of the past—what you have learned.

2. Spirit (Present): Your essence, the qualities of self that are in a state of evolution and development. The expression of the self in the here and now. Representing new or unrealized talents or abilities that have yet to be fulfilled—what needs to be activated.

3. Destiny (Future): A combination of the Soul and the Spirit, representing your Divine purpose. Like the "North Star," it is an inspiration to guide you. This placement is a goal that you are working toward achieving—what needs to be embraced to open your future.

THE LOVERS SPREAD

1. You in regard to the relationship: your expectations, hopes, and desires for the relationship

2. The person of your inquiry: how they perceive you, and what you represent to them

3. How you engage with one another: the essence of the relationship

4. What hinders the relationship: what needs to be resolved to move forward

5. The gift of the relationship: what you can learn from one another

6. The probable outcome: the potential for your future together

THE MOON SPREAD

The New Moon

The Crescent Moon

The Full Moon

The Waning Moon

THE MOON SPREAD

This spread is based on the different phases of the moon. A lunar cycle represents a beginning, middle, and end for a specific period of time. The Moon Spread can be used to review a creative process, reveal the development of a life situation, or express a reflection of an inner journey.

1. The New Moon: the beginning of a new cycle, what seeds need to be planted to achieve new dreams, your intention

2. The Crescent or First-Quarter Moon: a time for clarification, what needs to be cleared. Focus on nurturing and development.

3. The Full Moon: the situation reaches its apex or full development; what needs to be celebrated.

4. The Waning or Fourth-Quarter Moon: Darkness before rebirth, what to expect next, the process of preparing the new cycle